HOMEFRONT
WARRIORS

Not Every *Warrior* Wears A Uniform

CHANTEL OLSON

HOMEFRONT
WARRIORS

Not Every *Warrior* Wears A Uniform

CHANTEL OLSON

TABLE OF CONTENTS

INTRODUCTION: NOT EVERY WARRIOR WEARS A UNIFORM

If you're reading this, I suspect you probably fall into one of two camps—you are either a member of a military family, whether a soldier yourself or a soldier's spouse or relative—or you are someone who wants to know more about being "married to the uniform." In either case, I think it's important that as Americans, we are reminded of the sacrifice that goes into the freedoms we all enjoy.

We're all familiar with the "ultimate sacrifice" of soldiers giving their lives to protect their country and their families. You might not know it by looking at me, but I'm a big fan of war movies and being a soldier was going to be part of my future. And if it weren't for an injury I got while at officer training, I may have ended up as a career soldier. Funny thing is, in a way I still kind of did, and that is what this book is all about. You see, more sacrifices are required in fighting for freedom than traveling overseas and facing the enemy. Not every warrior wears a uniform.

Homefront Warriors means a lot of things to me. On one hand, it's a memoir that focuses mainly on a fifteen-month period when my husband, Jon, was deployed to Iraq. There were a lot of pivotal moments crammed into that short time frame that served as great learning opportunities for me. I attribute much of what happened during this time to the family we are today.

This book is also my opportunity to share my story (and that's exactly what it is—*my* story) and, in so doing, give others a voice. In the past few years, I have shared my experiences with people from all walks of life and have loved every minute of it. I speak publicly about many topics from my life, but talking about this story with other homefront warriors has always been special for me. I feel so connected to others when I speak about living as a military spouse and the trials, tribulations, and lessons that come from this. It is something I am so passionate about. And I'm reassured of how important sharing my story is when people I have never met approach me afterward and talk with me about their similar experiences. Having our experiences validated and given a voice is so powerful.

Perhaps most importantly, *Homefront Warriors* is a way for me to pass along the lessons I learned during and since the time my soldier was deployed. Some of these lessons come from what worked for me during that period of time; others are lessons I've learned since. My hope is that you can take something away from my story that will help you and your family.

I also want to be transparent and mention that there are a couple of things I was a little nervous about when it came time to write this book. First of all, I am writing it from the perspective of what it was like to be a homefront warrior, which isn't always easy. In no way do I mean to diminish the support of our US military or the support of their families. Even though I experienced some tough times, I have never resented or regretted our family's service to our country. I am extremely honored to have had the opportunity to serve as a homefront warrior. I wouldn't trade the pride I feel for anything.

Another concern for me is the current state of my marriage. After many years and two beautiful children, Jon and I are no longer together. We are still friendly with each other, and our split had nothing to do with his military service or the events covered in this book. I have no intention to portray him as anything other than the loving, caring man that he is.

I want my readers to know that the point my path has led to is not the ultimate ending of my story—it is still being written. Jon's homecoming was certainly a joyful moment for me, and I will always love and respect him. I feel blessed that our children still have a great relationship with me and with their father, and that our families are still close. Just because we are no longer together does not diminish the experiences I had or lessons I learned during his enlistment. It also doesn't lessen the sacrifices both of us made.

So what are homefront warriors? They're the people who stay behind; the ones who keep daily life running while their soldiers are away. Homefront warriors are my parents, who would look after my kids at a moment's notice and whose house was a place of acceptance and peace for me. Homefront warriors are my friends Kris and Judy, whose friendship and faith inspired and comforted me when I needed it most. They are people like Uncle Wes, who mowed my lawn without me having to ask, or Pastor Greg, who was always ready with a kind word and open arms. My children, Preston and Mary Louise, whose love and bravery gave me strength and a sense of purpose during a really difficult time. They are people like you, who keep things going despite the uncertainty and fear, who spend most days not knowing if you will see your loved one again but needing to go about life as though you will, who feel the need to stay strong even though part of you is missing. You are my heroes and I am eternally grateful.

I am equally grateful for Jon's service and for all soldiers abroad. The way I see it, the service we collectively offer is like a tree. Most of us are familiar with the service of the military men and women who dedicate their lives to our freedoms—we see them on the news, walking around in uniform, honored in parades. They are the trunk and limbs of the tree. The part that is most visible. Homefront warriors, on the other hand, are the roots. They are the support system that often goes unseen. Without the combined efforts of soldiers, with and without uniform, the freedoms we enjoy could not exist.

I hope my story offers encouragement and gives a voice to my fellow homefront warriors as well as an opportunity to notice and better support the homefront warriors in your life.

HOME FRONT

WARRIOR

Chapter 1

MARRIED TO
THE UNIFORM

Never in my wildest dreams did I think I would marry a soldier. My life plans looked very different—getting my dream job, traveling the world, and doing so without a husband or kids. But God has a special way of pointing us in the direction that we are meant to go. I met Jon on April 29, 1994, while in college, and at that time, he was serving in the National Guard. The following year, we were engaged and then married. I had no idea of the trials and tribulations that come with being married to the uniform, nor the extreme pride that emanates from it.

Shortly after we married, I could tell that Jon desperately wanted a child. This was the last thing on my mind.

Don't get me wrong, it's not that I was against having children; I just didn't feel like I was prepared to be a mother. I knew what military life was like. How could I do this by myself knowing that there would always be the chance of him being deployed? I felt very uncertain of my capabilities. I certainly didn't want to be a parent of a child without a father. To say the least, I was reluctant to start a family. I believe that deep down, I didn't want my children to go through those feelings of missing their father and have everything laid on my shoulders while still attempting to have a good marriage and create a good career. Of course, my understanding of the importance of both what my father did and what Jon wanted to do is much different than it was then—I completely understand their pride and commitment to the military and how important it is.

Luckily, after much discussion, Jon won that battle, and I am so glad that he did. But I needed to make a deal with him—I didn't believe I could have children *and* a husband in the military. I'm eternally grateful for my kids and wouldn't trade them for the world. But even then I knew what was in store for us if Jon were ever to be deployed overseas. I also knew he would make a great dad. If Jon wanted to start a family, the compromise was for him to not reenlist. He agreed, and for ten years we lived a "normal" life. He was a cop, I was a successful real estate agent, and we were blessed with two beautiful children—Mary Louise and Preston—whom I wouldn't trade for anything.

As our young family grew, I could see that something was still missing from Jon's life. He was always a great dad to our kids and a loving husband, but serving our country was his calling. After years of soul searching and prayer, Jon and I finally decided to give military life another try. I knew how much it meant to him and figured we would make it work. After all, Jon was mainly working nights by this point so I was used to handling a lot of things on my own. What I wasn't aware of at the time is the difference between being a single parent and having your partner missing from your life for periods of time, never knowing if or when he would return. In January of 2006, Jon reenlisted. I never knew how much my life would be impacted by this one seemingly small decision. My life as a military wife resumed.

A WARRIOR'S TRAINING

For those of you who have a loved one in the military, you are familiar with what it's like having this special person shipped off for all sorts of training, weeks or even months at a time. This is part of the sacrifice. This is what we signed up for. Thing is, the hardest part for me was watching our children cry every time they watched their father leave. It broke my heart each time.

Some of you even know what it's like to have this special person be gone for "family firsts." Preston's second birthday was one of these "firsts." At the age of two, Preston was presumably unaware of the missing piece of our day and what would be missing for the next few years. I, on the other hand, was all too sensitive to feeling the void, as if what was missing was a piece of me.

This was just the beginning. As many of you are familiar with, further training was required from that point, in which Jon had to be away from our family for months at a time. On one occasion, while he was stationed a long day's drive away, we went to see him for a couple of days. This was just enough to fill the kids' "Daddy tank" and to fill Jon's "family tank." When it was time to go, I was simply unprepared for what happened next. Standing by the car, Mary Louise and Preston started crying, wondering why Daddy couldn't come with us. I was simply devastated and didn't know what to do. This was going to be way harder than I had imagined.

While Jon was away for months of training, our lives continued. Mary Louise was in first grade. Preston was two and going part-time to day care. I was teaching for the South Dakota State University (SDSU) one night a week and rocking my real estate business full time. Needless to say, I stayed very busy trying to keep up with everything, but a piece of me was still missing. I felt extremely alone and completely overwhelmed in my jobs and in caring for my babies. But you never would have known it by looking at me.

You see, my way of coping was doing something I had learned to do long ago—building an emotional wall. "A wall?" you may ask. Yes, a wall—a wall guarding me from all emotion. I believed that as a mother I must always put on a brave face, no matter what the storm inside. I had to be strong for the kids. I had to hide my feelings of loneliness and abandonment. This had been *my* training.

A PIECE OF YOU IS MISSING

I remember so many nights while Jon was away at training, I would come home, make supper, do as much around the house as I could without stealing too much time from the kids. I would help Mary Louise with her homework, give baths, and get the kids into bed for nightly prayers. By the time I finally got to sit down, I was exhausted. By no means was my house immaculate or my children dressed to the nines, but I was doing the best I could given the circumstances.

As homefront warriors, we do our best while our soldier is away. We decide whether to vacuum the stairs or play with our kids. This is a constant dilemma for us. We get up and go to work. We do our best to raise our children without ever truly knowing the "right" way to do everything. And we do all of this while feeling as if a piece of us is missing and without knowing when it will return.

In the beginning, it was so difficult. My heart would ache because I knew that I couldn't have Jon next to me, hold his hand whenever I wanted, or just have the sense of security of knowing he was with me. But as time went on, I learned to be everything that I needed. I had to create my own sense of security, my own independence. I had to be the strong one for the kids even though deep inside, I was probably the weakest of all.

THE JIGGLE

These months as a single parent really brought to light the struggles and unexpected experiences that occur when you least expect them. As a parent, you never truly know the right way to do anything. Kids don't come with an instruction manual, but as a woman, I knew how to deal with my daughter and all of her "girl issues." I could teach her the correct manners for a young lady, and I knew how to potty train her, how to do her hair, etcetera. However, I was discovering just how different boys are to raise than girls.

For instance, boys have an inherent need to investigate each and every insect that may cross their path. Whether you are walking down the sidewalk, your family's going into church, or he is on the field playing T-ball, everything must stop in order for Preston to complete the investigation. Little boys have an infatuation with anything gross! I recall sitting on my stairway talking to my daughter when all of a sudden Preston came to me with dirty little hands. I know it doesn't seem out of the ordinary, but oh my! As I looked closer and did the "Mom sniff," I came to the realization that he had just discovered the litter box!

I would have to say that my favorite, yet most embarrassing, story comes from trying to potty train my son. He started later on the toilet training than my daughter had so I thought maybe he would understand things a bit better. I was wrong. As a woman, I was brought up to use toilet paper after using the bathroom for anything that happened on the "throne of knowledge." What I was unaware of was the routine that a boy needs to learn. Herein lied the problem and source of my, and soon to be my son's, embarrassment.

One afternoon, when I was picking Preston up from the day care center, the director pulled me aside. I was prepared for her to tell me that Preston had done something either extremely cute or very naughty. I wasn't sure which one it would be, but I braced myself for the worst. It turns out that I was wrong on both counts. She asked me, "Chantel, did you know that Preston uses a piece of toilet paper to wipe his front when he is done going potty?" Not knowing that it should be done any differently, I was confident in saying, "Yes! That is just how I taught him to do it." Well, apparently, that is not how it is done. Oops! It seems that there is a term that was missing from my vocabulary. It is called "the Jiggle!"

At that moment, I realized that this was going to be a long journey without Jon. How was I going to raise my son correctly without the guidance of someone who actually had the same equipment? Teaching my daughter was easy. I knew how everything worked. My son, however, did not come with an instruction manual.

A few months later, I was showing a house to some friends and had brought Preston along. Preston had never met my friend's husband, but I noticed him clutching to his leg as if he knew him. When we were over at my parents' house, Preston stuck to my dad like glue. Everywhere we went, Preston would gravitate toward a man. He yearned for a male figure so badly that even a stranger seemed an adequate replacement to his own father. My heart broke for him when I recognized I could never give him the one thing he needed most. No matter how great of a mom I was, no matter how much I loved him, I could never fulfill that role for my son. I realized yet again that this was going to be a long journey without Jon.

TOUGH DECISIONS

Once Jon's training was complete, we found out where he was going to be stationed. I remember the call from Jon quite vividly. On my way to a showing, I was feeling great about everything I'd been accomplishing—building a successful real estate business while teaching and raising the kids all on my own. I felt on top of the world. But this feeling of accomplishment was quickly offset by the feeling that we were about to lose everything. He was going to be stationed six hours away in Fort Riley, Kansas.

Don't get me wrong, I was really happy for Jon and proud of everything he had accomplished. But the idea of moving away from my support system really took the wind out of my sails. We had moved about a year and a half earlier, and the kids were finally feeling somewhat stable. They had gotten really close with my parents. This was certainly going to shake them up a bit. With the news of where our solder would be stationed, our family was left with a very difficult decision. Should my children and I continue living in South Dakota without Jon? Or should we move to an entirely new place and start all over?

We started off by driving down to see Jon on the weekends until Mary Louise was done with school for the summer. Then we made a partial move to Kansas. A day into the new school year, we heard that Jon would be deployed for at least twelve months. As much as I wanted to be together as a family, I wanted my kids to have a stable environment and a permanent home; I felt torn. We didn't know a soul in Fort Riley, and we felt the kids would be better off back in South Dakota. It wouldn't be easy for Jon and me, but we thought we were doing the best for the kids.

As homefront warriors, these are the types of tough decisions we are faced with—raise our children in a community of people they know even if it means being away from their father or uproot them for only a hope that they could see their father before he's deployed. Looking back on it, as hard as it was, I'm glad we made the decision to keep them in our South Dakota home.

It wasn't long after we left Fort Riley to return home that I received another phone call from Jon. This time it was a deployment warning, which basically meant Jon's unit might be shipped out at any time. While the discomfort and unknowns of deployment were looming, I was grateful that Mary Louise could return to her school and her friends, and I had my family and support system already in place.

This may not be the decision other soldiers and homefront warriors would make for their own families. And it may not even be the "best" choice. But we made the choice we felt was best given our circumstances, and it worked out, in many ways, in our favor.

As homefront warriors, we are faced with tough decisions such as these all the time. And whether or not you have children, when your soldier is away, it's as if a piece of you is missing. For me, this meant that I did the best I could with the information I had, raised my children without their father for long periods at a time, kept the house in order despite the feelings of chaos, and worked a full-time job, all the while feeling this void. And what often makes it harder for us is that while our loved ones are missing from our lives, there is also a constant sense of not knowing what to be prepared for next.

Chapter 2

LIVING
IN LIMBO

The kids and I had just moved back to South Dakota and we were making weekend trips to visit Jon while we waited to learn more about his deployment. At this point, I had so much of a wall built around my heart that it didn't even seem to bother me when we said our good-byes. I just made it look as though I would see him later, no big deal. This was how effective my training had been.

We settled back into our routine and I did the best I could to "keep myself together." My emotional wall was becoming fortified, brick by brick. I truly believed that if I showed emotion, my kids would see it and suffer more. Even though I was dying inside of loneliness and heartache, I tried to wear my mask of "Everything is fine!" and go about life as though all was as it should be. But it was a lie. I hated going through this.

It tore me to pieces when Preston would cry those big crocodile tears at the end of each visit. And even though Mary Louise was a bit older now and didn't show as much emotion, I could see her sadness as well. I just hated seeing my babies go through that. I felt I was unsuccessful in my efforts to shield them from these hard parts of life and the accompanying heartache.

For each of us homefront warriors, there are so many unknowns regarding what is to come that seeing our soldiers for short spurts of time is necessary for all of us. The uncertainty of the impending deployment takes quite a toll on us and our children. My approach was to fill their "Daddy tank" and prepare as best I could. But there are just some things you can't prepare for.

THE CALL

Have you ever had a feeling of just knowing something terrible was going to happen, so you went ahead and mentally prepared for it? You know it is going to happen—you are just waiting for that fateful moment to arrive. Well, that is what it was like for me the night I received the official call.

For months we had been preparing for the time Jon would have to leave. This meant I coped with the stress the only way I knew how—I kept all of the fear, chaos, and uncertainty trapped behind my emotional wall and away from my kids. I tried not to talk about it around them but got things done without their knowledge. It was more difficult than one might think. Making sure all insurance was up to date, all paperwork in order, everything planned and accounted for. My training was effective—or so I thought.

I often compare my wait for the dreaded call to having a loved one with a terminal illness—there's only one outcome, it's horrible, and you know it's going to happen, but you are never quite as prepared for that fateful moment as you think.

That evening, after putting the kids to bed and saying our prayers, I sat in the living room, lights down low, in silence. And that's when it happened. The phone rang. It was a Kansas number. The woman on the other end introduced herself as a member of the Family Readiness Group, the wife of another soldier. She continued to say, "I am calling you to let you know that your soldier has been activated for the fifteen-month surge in Iraq." My heart sank. I sat there in the dark with my body frozen. It was as though someone had paralyzed me with just one sentence. I don't remember much else of what she said after that. I vaguely recall uttering some default responses such as "Uh-huh" and "Yeah, okay" before hanging up the phone.

I thought my wall could handle the news, but it hit me like a ton of bricks. Had we stayed in Fort Riley, I might have been able to talk it out with another spouse I had just met. I might have taken advantage of the community of military families. But this was the decision I had made. And now I was all alone. Inside, my heart wrenched.

This is really happening. The phrase kept replaying in my head. I could almost feel the switch inside my brain flip to "Military Mode." There in my living room, sitting by myself in the dark, I prayed for the strength to get my family through this. The next morning, I didn't tell

Preston and Mary Louise their daddy would be leaving. I wouldn't tell them for another two weeks. Life had to go on, and I had to keep it going. The only thing I knew how to do was fortify my emotional wall even more and plan for what was next.

PREPARE FOR THE WORST,
PRAY FOR THE BEST

Over the next few weeks, I started getting things in order for the impending deployment. There was now an encyclopedia of preparations to add to my already busy life. There was your typical JAG paperwork—the power of attorney, the will—not to mention needing Jon to write a "final letter" to us in case of the unforeseen. It felt like I was signing away my husband. These are the thoughts and realities we homefront warriors have to face head-on.

This became very real for me the Sunday before Jon's deployment. We gathered at a Sioux Falls hotel for Preston's third birthday party. I watched Preston playing with Jon, and my heart ached at the thought of how much my little boy loved his daddy and how much he'd miss him in only two days' time. I couldn't get the terrible thought out of my head that this could be the last time my friends or family would ever see Jon. I was feeling quite numb with anticipation, fear, and a whole lot of faith. Anticipation for what was to come, fear of what could possibly happen, and faith that God would bring me through this.

After the party that evening, we loaded up the Jeep and headed south to Kansas. Most people who saw us wouldn't have realized that this wasn't your typical family vacation or road trip. You see, military families have to plan for so many things that other families don't usually need to worry about. We weren't just sending Daddy off on a work trip for a week or two. We were sending him off to a foreign country, in the middle of a war zone, and we wouldn't see him again for fifteen months. During the trip down, I wanted to cry so many times. I was so scared. The thought of living without him for that long was torture.

Even though I knew it was nearly impossible that Jon's deployment would get called off, I held out hope until the very last moment. Always the optimist, I guess. Please don't get me wrong. I was very proud of what we were making this sacrifice for; it was our duty and what Jon had trained so hard to do. But when it comes to looking out for your family, one can only pray.

We spent our first day in Kansas shopping for a few things to help us prepare. Among these was a video camera so we could send videos of Mary Louise singing in church and Preston doing cute toddler things to Jon while he was away. After spending a few hours together at Chuck E. Cheese letting the kids play and making a few more memories, we needed to make one more purchase—one I was not looking forward to because it symbolized so much.

A MEMENTO

Even with all the fun we were having, we still had one daunting task left to complete. As terrible as it may sound, there was an image I had been dwelling on for the last few weeks and that wouldn't subside: a soldier stripped of all his clothes and belongings and dragged around the city. What would happen if my soldier was captured? Would they do the same to him? I couldn't even imagine. And the thing that kept haunting me was that I didn't want Jon's wedding ring to fall into the hands of the enemy. He, however, wanted to wear his ring, so we had to come to some sort of a solution.

Our final task was to buy Jon a stand-in ring. It was one of the hardest things I have ever had to do. I remember standing over the jewelry counter next to Jon looking at the rings. So many to choose from, but I didn't want to have to choose. It was too much. I told Jon to pick out the one he wanted. My heart was sick, my eyes fighting back the tears. I just stood there, barely able to move, while he tried them on. He chose a plain gold band. We kept his original wedding ring at home for safekeeping. This way if, God forbid, something happened, Preston would be able to have his Daddy's ring. I often wore his ring while he was gone—sometimes on a chain, sometimes around my thumb. Just feeling the mold of his finger was enough to give me that connection point, to feel like he was still there with me.

Again, this probably isn't something most families need to think about, but soldiers and their families understand the need to preserve memories of their loved ones. With the fear and uncertainty that comes with sending off your loved one, holding onto a memento is one of the few ways we know to prepare for the worst while praying for the best.

Chapter 3

NEEDING TO "STAY STRONG"

W e spent the evening before Jon's deployment at the lodging in Fort Riley. The mood was quite different than it had been earlier that day. It was a bit more somber with us knowing what was to come. My mind was a flurry of what-to-do's, what-if's, and how-will-I-ever's. But the biggest concern on my mind, other than the safety of my husband, was how in the world I would make the six-hour drive home after the day we would have tomorrow.

I called my parents that evening to check in. Mom must have had her radar on because she could tell from my voice that something wasn't right. I just couldn't stop thinking of the drive back home. I would have to drive through the night to get Mary Louise to school the next day. I would have to do it alone and running on three hours of lousy sleep. It may not sound like a daunting task under normal circumstances, but as many home-front warriors know, sending off your soldier is a quite distressing, emotionally draining event. I kept asking myself, "How will I get my babies home safely?" I came to the conclusion that I had to put on my big girl panties and push through yet again and pray that God would give me the strength to overcome.

As it got later and closer to bedtime, I got a sinking feeling in the pit of my stomach. The thought finally hit me that tomorrow I would be saying good-bye to my husband, my lover, and my friend. It's true that we had spent the last year pretty much apart and on our own, but this was different. There would be no weekend visits, no picking up the phone to call him whenever I wanted or needed to.

That night was agony. I was completely exhausted but I just lay there, listening to Jon's heartbeat. I knew I needed to sleep, but I just couldn't. I lay there in Jon's arms, feeling his breath on my neck—I didn't want to miss a moment of these last precious minutes together. My chest was tight, my throat even tighter, from trying to hide my feelings. I prayed so hard that night. I prayed that God would bring him home to us safely. I prayed that I would be strong enough.

This was my way of handling things. Suck it up. Power through. Don't show emotion. To me, this is what it meant to be strong. What I was yet to learn is that true strength means something entirely different.

UNEXPECTED GIFTS

February 7, 2007, will forever be carved into my heart. It was D-Day: Deployment Day. Our lives would be forever changed. I had been dreading this day for quite some time and now it had come. The day began early so we could get ready and tie up any loose ends. I was not myself. I was going through the motions but didn't really take into account what was actually happening. My mind was far, far away. I knew that this would be our last day together for a while. I was going through this emotional storm inside, but felt I had to be the strong one.

Have you ever heard the saying "God will never give you more than you can handle"? Well, He must have realized that I was near my breaking point because He sent His angels to lift one of the biggest burdens of the day for me.

Not very long after we woke up, I got a call from my parents. At first, I was a little concerned that something was wrong, but no. They were calling to answer my prayers. "We are on our way and only a couple of hours out!" My eyes filled with tears of joy, relief, and sadness all at once. There was nothing I needed more at that moment than my parents.

These wonderful angels knew I was overburdened and worried about the return drive home and the safety of my children. If that isn't love and a gift from God Himself, I don't know what is. I had much to face that day, but this blessing gave me the strength to endure what was to come—strength in the form of offering and receiving help.

Before Jon needed to get to formation, we had a few more items to pick up from the local store. While we were shopping, a nice lady approached us. Jon was in full uniform; I looked a wreck with red, swollen eyes; and we had two kids in tow. This kind woman wanted to thank Jon for his service. We told her it was his deployment day, and she slowly reached into her pocket to grab something. She then handed Jon three dollars. "I don't have much, but I want to give you something." Nothing like this had happened to us before and we didn't know what to do. Jon immediately tried to give it back to her, but she insisted he keep it. "It's my way of giving back for what you are about to sacrifice."

Small gestures like hers are what keep families like mine going. I understand most people who saw us that day probably didn't want to interfere. Perhaps they figured that leaving us in peace was the polite thing to do. I speak for many homefront warriors when I say we wouldn't have turned away any kind word that day. To me, random acts of kindness such as that woman's are worth millions. It filled my heart with so much joy and helped me feel seen and understood on such a difficult day. It reminded me that we weren't going through all of this alone.

SAYING GOOD-BYE

The deployment time was quickly approaching so we headed back to the post. This was an extremely quiet and nerve-racking drive. We met my folks in the parking lot, which was filled with buses and families taking pictures and saying good-bye. We then took a few photos of our own and said our good-byes. I wanted so badly not to cry for fear of how the kids would react, but I was simply not able to hold in my tears any longer. When I saw Preston lay his little head on his Daddy's shoulder, tears tumbled down my face as I prayed that Jon would come back safely.

February 7, 2007, was a somber day for all of us. My greatest relief was having the support of my parents and their help getting us home safely. I didn't realize it at the time, but I was learning a very important lesson—the importance of receiving help and tearing down my emotional wall, brick by brick.

This lesson, however, would take a while to learn. In the meantime, I constantly convinced myself that everything was going to be all right, even when I didn't believe it. I had my emotional wall and I had my kids. My kids were now my sense of purpose, and I was going to get them through this.

FORTIFYING MY WALL

Once the kids and I returned home, life continued on, but the atmosphere was different. The kids and I went about our well-established routine as best we could with a few bumps along the way.

This is where that wall I had been building came into play. No matter how high or thick I stacked those bricks, something would inevitably trigger me. I just prayed I would always be alone when it happened. Sometimes, I'd hear a song on the radio and the emotion I felt would become too much to bear. Military commercials to this day are very emotional for me. That sense of sacrifice and loss is all too real. As time passed, my emotional wall became very effective at deflecting most of these blows.

I recall one moment in particular when I recognized just how fortified my wall had become: when I received the first call from Jon while he was in Baghdad. I was so excited to hear his voice and know that he was okay. As our conversation carried on, I heard something in the background on his end. My heart pounded. "Is that what I think it is?"

"Yes," he answered. It was a bomb and some explosions going off.

I then asked, in a remarkably calm voice, "Is that incoming or outgoing?"

Not a conversation most people have with their spouse. This was how much of a wall I had built around my heart. I responded as though it didn't even faze me. On the inside, I remember being terrified, but I couldn't bring myself to show it. It was important that I stay strong for Jon to give him peace of mind. He couldn't do his job abroad if he was worried about me and how I was feeling. Looking back on it now, I wonder if Jon needed me to show a little more emotion and fear. But I was afraid to show what I then considered weakness.

During Jon's deployment, I went about my life as though Preston and Mary Louise were solely dependent on me. This is what it's like as a homefront warrior—not knowing when or if your loved one will return, or in what condition. I had to keep it all together by myself. Not only was I working day and night, but I also had to make time for my children and their activities, keep up the house, and be ready to put out any other fires that required my attention. I was completely exhausted most of the time, but I believed I had to continue to be strong and keep going. I never told anyone at the time, but I went through a terrible depression for several months. Being the stubborn German that I am, I wouldn't ask for help. Having been so independent my entire life, I felt as though seeking assistance was a sign of weakness, and I certainly didn't want to appear weak.

I remember sitting alone in the living room one night with the lights down low, having just tucked the kids into bed, when I went into a trancelike state. It was as though I was in my own little world where nothing felt right. The future was uncertain; the road ahead seemed long and cumbersome. My friend, and confidant, was thousands of miles away. I felt so alone. So disconnected from the world. I wondered how I would get the strength to make it through just one more day.

Chapter 4

THE TWO FRONTS

W hen people think of military families, they often can't help but focus on the battle abroad. That is, the soldier's battle is the one most often asked about, prayed for, and discussed. This is totally understandable and not at all to be diminished. They are making huge sacrifices for us to have the freedoms we enjoy today. However, every warrior has his or her own battles to fight, and there is a second battle that is equally as important and oftentimes overlooked—the battle at home.

THE BATTLE AT HOME

While Jon was driving midnight convoys in Iraq, I was keeping our family together in Tea, South Dakota. A typical day for us, during that time of being without a husband and father, started with me waking up and trying to get as much done as possible before the kids got up. That usually didn't leave me much time because Preston was only three and an early riser, still very dependent on Mommy. I would start getting his toast ready so that he was eating when Mary Louise woke up so that I could then attend to her needs.

Once I got them fed and ready, I would take Mary Louise to school and Preston to day care. After the kids were dropped off, I could start my day at work. Pretty typical for most families at this point, but keep in mind that homefront warriors are doing all of this while fighting another battle. While the stresses of a single parent's life are very real, they didn't constitute my most difficult battleground. For many homefront warriors, the greatest conflict is fought within the mind.

The daily challenges of the soldier's family at home aren't something most people think about. In people's defense, though, we military families are usually good at hiding our own daily battles. Just look at me and my belief that I had to hold it together, stay strong, and pretend like everything was fine. At first glance, there's nothing that different about us. Our kids go to school and go out for sports. We live in neighborhoods. We blend in with the crowd. The battle we are fighting is less obvious but still very real. It's a battle of comparisons, guilt, worry, and daily sacrifices. It may not be easy, but it is a duty we can be proud to undertake.

FEELINGS OF ISOLATION

I felt Jon's absence the most at family gatherings. Every June, his family would meet in Okoboji for some swimming and outdoor fun. The kids would have a blast, but for me, it was tough being the only one there without a significant other. While others would talk about their families and spouses, all I did was sit there and listen, pretending everything was fine. The following month at my own family's Fourth of July reunion, it was more of the same. It was good to be there physically, but my heart wasn't there with me—it was with Jon.

With all of these conflicting feelings, and thinking that I had no one to talk to about them, I felt so hopelessly alone. My growing feelings of isolation didn't stop at family functions. For instance, we didn't receive invitations to people's houses or get phone calls the way we had before. I was quite puzzled and began feeling as if I had done something wrong.

What I later learned is that many people are apprehensive to be around families of soldiers because they don't know what to say or are afraid they might in some way upset us. I completely understand this concern. Deployment is a touchy subject as it is truly a life-or-death situation. But that doesn't make it easier for us homefront warriors. We are in such need of support and connection during this time. There are so many families affected by military deployments, and there are so many stresses and unimaginable hardships that go along with these.

I remember one homefront warrior who came up to me after I'd spoken at a women's event. She thanked me for echoing what she herself, as a military spouse, had gone through. "It was as if everyone just left us," she confided in me. "They didn't know what to say or do. They thought we were getting all this emotional support from the military." People assumed we didn't need any help, that our daily routines and brave smiles shielded us from losing a spouse. We, in turn, assumed they just didn't care about us. And nobody talked about it.

SACRIFICES MADE

Before Jon left, I had gone into real estate mainly because of the convenient scheduling. He'd still been a police officer then, working mostly nights and weekends, and I wanted one of us to be around at all times for Preston and Mary Louise. By the time he was deployed, I was doing really well for myself. I'm truly thankful when I think of how fortunate I was. Not all homefront warriors have the luxury of a flexible job. And yet, like most homefront warriors, I would still need to make sacrifices when it came to balancing my job with my children.

Though it would have been great to take my business to the next level, it would have cut into the time I had with Preston and Mary Louise. The way I saw it, they had already lost one parent, and I needed to be there for them now more than ever. I was teaching Monday night classes at SDSU in Sioux Falls to supplement our income. I enjoyed it for the most part, but it certainly didn't help with my ability to cope with the stress of everything and connect more with my kids. These were a couple of the many sacrifices I made as a homefront warrior.

Then, eight months into Jon's deployment, I was offered my dream job. I had put in an application for an organizer with a very large service organization just for fun and to see if I could get it. The job involved traveling around the country and working with entertainers. It sounded like a blast. It was what I had been waiting for my whole life. But there was no question—I couldn't take the job. Recognizing this was part of my service to my country didn't make turning it down any less devastating.

Another sacrifice homefront warriors make is for-feiting the figurative "shift change" that I always took for granted when Jon was home. This was made most obvi-ous when it came to moving heavy objects, mowing the lawn, and dealing with things I hated, like snakes. Then there were times when I just needed to lean on another person. I used to look forward to visiting my parents not only for a break from watching the kids but also for some adult conversation. I never realized just how much of a sacrifice it would be to go without simple, everyday dialogue.

COMPARISONS AND GUILT

I ran my household like clockwork. It wasn't a life-or-death situation like the one Jon was going through, but I saw it as an important way to serve my children. I was actively fighting a battle for order and stability, but it never felt as significant as the battle going on overseas.

I was constantly comparing my own struggle's with Jon's battle abroad. I couldn't help but think that however tough my day had been, his day had been worse. I kept telling myself that no matter how big my sacrifice, Jon's service was more important. After all, I was the one who got to stay home. I was there for birthdays, holidays, and countless milestones with the kids. But the wall was there too, keeping everything at arm's length. I was there for my children, but my mind was never completely in the moment; I was always worrying about the many what-if's that come with having a solider overseas. I felt an incredible amount of guilt knowing what he was going through so I could have these freedoms.

Why should I get to be with my family when Jon couldn't? What had I done to deserve peace and quiet when bombs were falling around the clock in Iraq? What did my sacrifice matter compared to the soldiers'? As I imagine applies to many homefront warriors, my obligations kept me from enjoying my family and my freedom. At the same time, my guilt kept me from proudly acknowledging that sacrifice. It was really the worst of both worlds.

I know now that we were both serving our country. I realize that a homefront warrior's sacrifice is just as great as the soldier's. But, in the moment, it can be hard to see this from the comfort of one's home. I felt a lot of guilt and wished that someone then had reminded me of the important sacrifice I was making each and every day. I was fighting for my family and doing the best I could to stay strong and be there for them. I'm proud to say I did just that. But looking back, I know asking for help would have saved me a lot of heartache.

Chapter 5

REDEFINING
STRENGTH

When you're in the military, you're constantly training. You train so much to do things automatically when the situation presents itself. But there was no official training for the loneliness and stress of being a homefront warrior. When Jon left, I had to rely on what I knew best: hard work, perseverance, and family above all else. This was my training. This was how I defined "strength." What I have learned in the many years since Jon's deployment is just how poorly that definition served me and my family at times. Luckily for me, plenty of people in my life were angels during my time of need and offered help without my having to ask for it. My only job was to be strong enough to receive it.

LEARNING TO RECEIVE

During the deployment and through all of the loneliness and stress, I turned to friends of mine. These incredible people are also homefront warriors—those who assist and look out for the families left behind. Without these wonderful people, our lives would have been even more difficult while our soldier was away.

Tom, our youth pastor, and his wife, Judy, were good friends of mine. They had four children, including one daughter who was the same age as Mary Louise. They also had a son who was much older than Preston, but he just loved having a boy to hang out with. They lived on a little acreage not far from us. Whenever we would spend time with them, it was as if time stood still. The kids would play and have so much fun together. As the kids were playing video games or making movies, we adults would just sit and talk. I don't know if they knew it, but I treasured that time dearly. I loved the peacefulness and the atmosphere there. Not only did they provide me with good company and conversation but they also helped with the kids. They were there when I couldn't get off work in time to get the kids or I had a house showing come up last minute and needed someone to watch them. I truly couldn't have made it through the deployment without them.

Another one of my warriors was my dear friend Kris. She and I have been friends for many years and have been through so much together. Her situation was similar to mine in that her husband was gone a lot as well. As a truck driver, he would be gone for weeks at a time, so Kris and I would offer each other moral support. She also had a son between the ages of Mary Louise and Preston. As with Tom and Judy, the kids would get to play and I would get the love and connection I needed during conversation with a dear friend.

Kris brought more than companionship to the table. I was able to drop by whenever I needed a friend or a last-minute sitter. I don't think many people realize how important it is to have someone who is there for you and your family at the drop of a hat.

THE POWER OF GIVING

As I was learning to receive from these vital and appreciated warriors, I also learned just how important it is to give. One afternoon, I was out mowing the lawn, taking advantage of a little free time while Preston was napping. I had met our elderly neighbors, Wendel and Harriet, before but had never taken the time to really get to know them. Wendel, at the time in his late eighties, strolled up to me while I was working.

"Do you know anyone who cooks around here?" he asked me. It took me a moment to understand what he was asking. I said, "You mean, a service like Meals on Wheels?"

"Well," he continued, "I'm kinda old and my wife is pretty crippled up and can't get around. I'm getting tired of sandwiches."

I smiled. It just so happened that I was cooking a roast in the crockpot that night. I told Wendel not to worry about dinner and said, "I'll call when supper is ready and I'm on my way over. I'll bring you each a plate!" I finished the lawn, went inside, and fixed up a plate of food.

It was a simple meal, but I felt excited about what I was doing. Something told me it would be a good idea to bring the kids with me so we marched up their driveway together. Wendel answered the door with a big smile, as though he had been waiting for us. As he showed us into their little kitchen, I noticed the elderly couple had already set out their placemats, plates, silverware, glasses, and evening pills. They seemed like a couple of kids on Christmas morning. This is when I realized that the excitement I felt was nothing compared to theirs.

After that, I would bring over food any time I grilled out or fixed a roast. It became an excuse for me to make cookies and bars to send over with the kids, which they absolutely loved! I would even buy a meal for each of them from our church's turkey supper from time to time. Their faces would light up every time we came over. I was helping them, but Wendel and Harriet were really saving me. We gave each other good company and caring conversation, but more than that, I was being healed by meeting their needs. It was a joy for me and helped me realize that sometimes giving is the greatest gift we can receive.

Take it from me: it isn't always easy for homefront warriors to ask for help, as Wendel did with me. Giving of yourself to someone else in need is a great way to learn to receive. If you can find a way to share the fruits of your labor, you'll find that you're helping yourself as well. You may be surprised just how much healing it can bring to you and your family.

LEARNING TO HAVE NEEDS

One Sunday after church, Pastor Greg came up to me holding a piece of folded paper. On it, scribbled in crayon, was a letter written by my three-year-old Preston. *Dear God*, it read, *we love you very much. Can you please bring our daddy home?* He had written it during the sermon that morning and had given it to Pastor Greg with instructions to deliver it to God. It broke my heart and showed me something I hadn't considered before.

I could protect my children from most dangers. I could be there for them and help them like any good mom, but I could never protect them from the pain they felt. But boy did I try. I thought by not showing my own emotion, I could save them from feeling their own sadness. I thought I had to be strong for my kids. If they saw me sad or downtrodden, they may start to feel the same way and miss Daddy even more. One of my main concerns over the course of Jon's deployment was "How am I going to handle this with the kids?" My love for them was, and still is, stronger than any love I have ever felt. I thought I would be devastated if I didn't handle this whole thing correctly and brought more suffering upon my children. I was determined to take the brunt of this experience in whatever way I could.

What I didn't realize at the time was the impact "being strong" and "taking the brunt" was having on my children. Sometimes I showed so little emotion that it appeared to the kids that I was cold-hearted and unfeeling. Little did they know I was exhausted and dying inside. I would have loved to let myself go a little more, but I felt I couldn't. Looking back on it now, I did my children a disservice. They didn't get the whole picture, and for that, I am sorry.

In addition, because I never gave myself permission to have needs, I know there were times I was short with my kids. I was on edge most of the time. I realize that recognizing my own needs for help and affirmation would have lessened my daily stress. Had I been strong enough to ask for the help I needed, my children would have had a more relaxed and attentive mom. Of equal importance, I could have spent more time with them. By shouldering the burden all on my own, I had set myself up to feel alone and my children to feel that I didn't care as much as I truly did.

My hope is that my story and lessons invite other homefront warriors to redefine strength for themselves and learn other ways of coping with the loneliness and stress that are an inevitable part of the job. What I learned is that you don't have to go it alone or act tough all the time. I might have even been stronger had I done things differently.

Redefining strength for me means asking for help when it's needed, expressing what I'm going through, carving out space and time to grieve, and receiving random acts of kindness from others with grace and gratitude. I now see how much of a difference it would have made for me to break down my emotional wall sooner to let myself ask for the help I needed, much as Wendel did with me, and to let myself go a bit more when it came to how I was feeling. Maybe then it would have been a little easier to navigate the relationships in my life that meant the most to me.

Chapter 6

NAVIGATING RELATIONSHIPS

About thirteen months into Jon's surge, I received some good news along with some that was not so good. The good news was Jon was coming home early. The bad news was why: he had been diagnosed with skin cancer. It wasn't terribly serious, though at the time it was quite worrying to me. The cancer was isolated to a small area on the bridge of his nose. Apparently, even the sunshine in Iraq was hostile.

COMING HOME

Jon's homecoming was a bit different than what most soldiers experience, and it was certainly nothing like the movies. When he returned, I flew down to Fort Sam in Houston, Texas, by myself to meet Jon at the hospital there. The joy I felt at finally seeing him was mixed with feelings of appreciation for just how fortunate I was. As we embraced, I couldn't help but notice the wounded soldiers around us and think just how lucky Jon had been. There were so many soldiers in wheelchairs, in much worse shape than Jon.

The day of Jon's surgery, I remember sitting with him outside while we waited for the test results. As we sat and talked, I saw a young woman wheeling in her soldier. The man's body had been reduced to a torso with one arm. In that moment, I felt extremely blessed and grateful to have my solder back in one piece. Witnessing the sacrifice of so many heroes around you as I did, you can't help but feel blessed with your own lot in life.

The surgery was a success, and I flew home the next day. Jon didn't think he could make it home in time for Easter as he still had two weeks of debriefing left. There was also the matter of asking permission from his superiors. Plus, the doctors at Fort Sam Houston needed to make sure the melanoma was gone for good. I knew

Jon hated asking for favors, but I told him how much it would mean to me. To our surprise, a four-day visit was approved. Preston and Mary Louise would have their daddy home for Easter.

The kids were so excited when we met him at the airport. Everyone was in tears when Jon stepped off the plane. It was like that perfect homecoming scene from the movies, almost as if we had been given a do-over. Preston and Mary Louise fastened themselves to their daddy's legs and it looked as though they'd never let go. We were a family again.

After that, we just went home. Nothing special, no big party. We had over some family members and just hung out. I wouldn't have asked for anything different. I was enjoying being whole once again and watching the kids get reacquainted with Jon. When Jon had left, Preston had just turned three. He was now four and two months. Mary Louise had also matured quite a bit since Jon's deployment. After more than a year without his family, he was finally back in our lives.

For the next several months, Jon still lived and worked in Kansas, and we resumed our weekend trips.

The kids were ecstatic. I was grateful, proud, excited, and honestly looking forward to having someone to talk with. All of us were eager to get back to a normal life. I never once stopped to think just how difficult this would turn out to be.

TWO WORLDS COLLIDE

I had run a tight ship while Jon was away. This was my way of providing for my children and being a reliable mother. At first it seemed as though the principles of discipline that Jon and I shared would run parallel to one another. In my eyes, daily routines and meals were run like clockwork. Jon, on the other hand, was used to being his own person. Military life came with a strict sense of purpose during shifts and an earned reward of downtime in between. I, on the other hand, was expected to be everything for everyone … all the time. There are no shifts for homefront warriors, and there certainly isn't any downtime.

During his deployment, all Jon had retained of his family was what he remembered leaving behind. But things did not stand still while he was away. The kids and I had to change a great deal and make a lot of sacrifices to keep things running smoothly. By the time he got home, the life Jon had left behind was in a completely different environment. Jon was a stranger in his own house. The kids had changed drastically; the way we functioned as a family had evolved.

Around the first week after he got back, Jon put his foot down while we were all out for a drive. "Now that I'm home," he barked, cutting off the laughter coming from the backseat, "things are going to change. You kids are going to start behaving." At the time, it hit me like a slap to the face. I know now Jon was just trying to establish something that resembled order in his life. He never meant to hurt me. But all I heard was disappointment in my job as a parent—the assertion that he was here to fix all my mistakes. I had done the best I could. I thought I had raised Preston and Mary Louise to be caring, respectful kids. For fourteen months, my life had been defined by my children and I was proud of that. All of that went out the window in an instant.

Our worlds were quickly beginning to collide.

EXPECTATIONS ON BOTH SIDES

Homefront warriors and soldiers alike should expect some level of friction during the first few months of a homecoming. Part of coming to terms with any potential conflict is recognizing the expectations of everyone involved. You may find that your idea of "normal" and your spouse's may not sync up anymore.

The most important thing to remember is to *give it time*. It's impossible for anyone to instantly adjust to a new way of living, especially one so different from military life. Soldiers must remember that they are loved and appreciated by their families—that their friends and family are excited to have them back. But homecoming soldiers are entering an environment that has had to change while they were away. Things won't be the same as they left them because people aren't static. The sacrifices we homefront warriors make to compensate for the absence of our soldiers changes every aspect of our lives.

When Jon came home, I was expecting to get back my husband, just the way I remembered him. He, in turn, had expected the changes that had happened in his absence to adjust to his way of thinking. These assumptions were equally skewed. Preston and Mary Louise had grown, matured, and done so much that year. In turn, I had changed to keep up with all of that. Jon had experienced a year of war. I knew it would be an adjustment. He was going to be a changed man.

This became very real to me when we were visiting him in Kansas over the Fourth of July. While staying in our fifth-wheel camper, a firework went off nearby. The sound of this sent Jon to the floor. In this moment, I knew just how much of an adjustment it would be. There was a real need for patience and understanding for both of us.

My expectations of Jon were just as unreasonable as his expectations of me. I knew he would be a different man; I just didn't know how different. In reality, he hadn't changed that much—but it seemed that way because of how much we, out of necessity, had changed ourselves. I'm sure he wasn't expecting to come home to find that his wife had built an emotional wall around herself. The entire time he was home, I couldn't enjoy myself. I just kept thinking *when is he going to leave again?* from behind my tough exterior. Both of us were guilty of interpreting the other person's mood as something unwelcomed. We both felt out of control in an environment that had changed too quickly and would never be quite the same again.

It was the quality, not the frequency, of our conversations that brought all of this to light. And breaking through the silence to that understanding brought about the first signs of healing to my family. Being able to be fully present to the moment and how I'm feeling is still an ongoing practice for me. The difference between now and then is I've finally given myself the time needed to reflect on and reconcile those fifteen months.

HEALING RELATIONSHIPS

Everyone had grown during this time frame. Personalities and ways of thinking change for both soldiers and their families. It takes a long time to take everything in. It's okay to allow yourself the time needed to get to know each other again. The ideal situation would be to plan for this re-acclimation before the deployment, making some sort of counseling a part of the initial planning. This could be marriage, family, or military counseling; any kind will be a great help. But I know firsthand that it can be difficult to ask for that help. What I've learned is setting aside the time to speak with an objective third party is the best way to gain perspective from each other.

This is not an admittance of failure or weakness on anyone's part. I get it: it's a lot harder to ask for help than to just tell yourself you're fine and push through. It takes a lot of courage to reach out. Even if you go only once or twice, talking with someone about your experiences is going to help your relationships. It may be the only way many people are able to really *hear* their loved one's story instead of just listening. Everyone in the family can benefit.

Integrating counseling sessions into the planning phase may be difficult for some. As many homefront warriors know, there are a ton of boxes to check on the list of things to do before your soldier is deployed. If you can't plan ahead, my suggestion is to take the time a day or two after your soldier returns to sit down as a family and talk it out. It's best for everyone if all family members can admit up front that reintegrating your soldier is going to be tough. There are going to be bumps along the way, but you can get through it if you're in it together. If something's eating at you, don't just let it go. Say something. Talk it out. In my experience, these little frictions are only going to fester if they aren't addressed. You owe it to yourself, your family, and your soldier to identify problems before they manifest in the home.

Chapter 7

GETTING
SUPPORT

.

During your soldier's deployment, you'll find a great many things will change—not just your relationships. You may not have thought about some of these factors. It becomes clear very early on that your soldier's absence is really the tip of the iceberg when it comes to life changes. As we've explored in this book, homefront warriors deal with a lot of chaos, uncertainty, needing to be strong for others, making sacrifices, learning how to ask for help, and learning how to reintegrate as a family.

Through my story, I hope that both homefront warriors and everyday civilians come to better understand the types of support to ask for, and offer, knowing the many challenges that can arise.

A HELPING HAND

It's important for people to understand that military families don't always want to be left alone. We are people just like you. When our soldiers are deployed, we need our family and friends more than ever. And I completely understand how some people have a hard time asking for help. It was nearly impossible for me. But having friends and family show up and connect made a world of difference for me. And that old line "Let me know if you need anything" can feel like more of a burden than a comfort to most military families. We aren't always clear on what it is we need exactly. My advice to those wanting to offer help is just do it.

If you know dropping off a lasagna would mean the world to a single parent, just do it. If mowing the lawn, arranging for a babysitter, or extending an invitation to coffee would be a blessing to someone, please just do it. Some people may have an easier time asking for the things they need, but what I've learned is most people won't, or are too busy to realize they need it. I remember thinking how wonderful it would have been for a maid to come and clean for one day. Just to have someone drive me somewhere for a change would have been incredible. That brief moment of rest would have meant so much to me. Since I wasn't accustomed to asking for help, one of the simple gestures I've named would have been a miracle! And that's all it takes to help your local homefront warrior.

Another great help to me were the people in my life who didn't just listen but *understood* what I was going through. As I mentioned before, my friend Kris's husband, Brett, is a truck driver so she understood what it meant to be a single parent. She may not have gotten the whole "military" aspect of my life but she listened and was there for me. I found so much solace in her and her family. Additionally, I always had my mom and dad to talk with, and they were always eager to help with the kids. We may not have talked about it much, but I knew they understood what it meant to be married to the uniform.

With their combined compassion, I had a support group who took the time to understand my daily battles.

Equally, if you are a military spouse, I highly urge you to find a person or group of people in your life who have compassion for you. Knowing that everything is going to be okay and that you'll get through it makes so much difference. Whether with other military spouses or a support group, making that connection with those who understand is integral to the battle at home. Don't be afraid to seek out good listeners and, alternatively, don't be afraid to offer your ear to your own local homefront warriors.

FINDING SANCTUARY

Another important area of support is finding a sanctuary—a place where you feel relieved and at ease. Church was one of those places for me. With all of the chaos going on in my life, my head, and my heart, the moment I walked into that building, a feeling of calm came over me.

Trinity Lutheran Church in Tea, South Dakota, is a simple brick building. If you were to look at it, you'd see the additions that, over the years, transformed a simple chapel into a huge fellowship hall. The grounds around the parking lot and the welcome sign are well kept. There's even a small garden in the back. But the feature that speaks to me the most is a rock with these words engraved on its surface: "Leave your burdens at my door."

Fighting the battle within my mind—this battle for certainty, comfort, and peace—would have been impossible without my hometown church. It was a place I could actually stop, breathe, and allow myself an hour or two to just let go. It was a place free from judgment, obligation, and stress. As soon as I walked through those doors, everything suddenly felt right. I knew Preston and Mary Louise were safe, I didn't have to think about work, and my priorities were straightened out. Going to church was a highlight of my week. Sometimes, we would go both Sunday morning and Wednesday night. While many of my daily worries were still with me, they felt so much lighter in that space. Here, I found an escape from feeling my heart stop each time the doorbell rang.

Perhaps one of the greatest gifts my sanctuary gave me was the permission to grieve. I cried a lot at church. It seemed like the only appropriate time and place to step out from behind my wall. Being reminded of His sacrifice for the world never failed to put life in perspective for me. But even beyond that, church was a place for me to be still and rest. I know religion may not be for everybody, but I strongly encourage all homefront warriors to seek out your own place of solace. Having this sacred space to feel, grieve, and relax is so important.

Finding that quiet, calm sanctuary is a necessary piece to fulfilling your spiritual relationship. Church was a place of great community for me. Pastor Greg, along with the youth director and their families, was always there to look after us and offer up a word of grace to me. Again, your sanctuary doesn't have to be a literal church sanctuary. Some may find their center in meditation or exercise. I recommend finding a place where you feel safe, a place where you don't have to think or try so hard, a place where you can just be. For me, that kind of relief gave me the solace I needed to keep going.

COVERING ALL YOUR BASES

There is no substitute for having your soldier home and in your life. But looking back, I realize that I just wasn't fully prepared for how much this would impact me. Many of the challenges faced by homefront warriors that I've talked about in this book are foreseen and partially preventable. I realize had we chosen to uproot and move to Fort Riley, I may have had the benefit of a community who understood these instabilities and offered me some relief from a few of these challenges. Equally, I understand living in post housing won't be for every military family, just as it wasn't for ours. Whichever you choose, a little preparation goes a long way. It can be a lifesaver.

Knowing what I know now, I can confidently say that the ideal situation is to sit down together and set things up ahead of time. But most importantly, do this *as a family*. I cannot stress enough how important it is to get everyone involved in planning your soldier's deployment. Communication is key throughout all of this. With my children being the ages they were, I never really sat down with them before or after Jon's deployment and talked things through. I relied on what I did best and kept things to myself, hoping this would somehow protect me and my children. I figured everything would be fine. I would figure it out. We would just go with the flow. That was a mistake.

I remember a friend of mine telling me her soldier had planned everything for her while he was away. And I do mean everything. He had called ahead to all the utility companies and scheduled routine maintenance on their home and car. Her soldier had asked his friends to drop by on a regular basis and help with chores and other tasks. He had even prepurchased flowers to be delivered for their anniversary.

I won't lie. This would have made my life much, much easier. But you should know that even a little planning could make a huge difference. Talk to your neighbors and friends. Plan for nights out and babysitters ahead of time. Surround your homefront warrior with a system of caring people and make sure that everyone knows what to expect. If you can identify even a few major needs while your soldier is away, you are more likely to receive help when you need it most. Plan for those moments when you know you'll be lonely. Talk with your friends about how often you'd like to socialize. Meet with your church leaders or community to help think of spiritual needs you may not have thought of before.

My best advice is, again, to bring those closest to you into the planning process as much as possible. Friends and neighbors who know what to expect are more likely to provide a homefront warrior with the encouragement and inclusiveness needed when times are toughest. A friend like Kris and supportive people like my parents, who understand even a bit of what you're going through, are invaluable to a homefront warrior. Being able to help one another and talk things out is a great stress outlet.

Also, remember to stick close to your family during these times. For me, feeling Preston and Mary Louise's little kisses each morning kept me going. My kids were, and still are, my power source. But make sure you know the difference between your sources of power and your outlets for recharging. It's okay if you need multiples of each. "Everything is fine!" won't cut it. I learned that the hard way. Your friends and family need to know what you're going through—and you need to be the one to tell them. You can save your heart and your family a lot of trouble by seeking the support you need and addressing as much of it as possible, as early as possible.

CONCLUSION:
SUSTAINING VICTORY

Even though my emotional wall is still standing, I've begun taking it down, brick by brick. It's still hanging around from those early months of loneliness, when my feelings of abandonment were strongest. Even writing this book now, I'm realizing just how many feelings I had buried in the mortar of my wall. It's been a tough process, but it's also given me an incredible amount of introspection. The days that felt like years, the mental anguish, the constant "hurry-up-and-wait" lifestyle of a military spouse reinforced the foundations of my emotional wall. And you know what? It's okay that it's taken this long to dismantle it. I just have to remind myself I'm still writing the end of my story.

A HAPPY ENDING

The idea of writing this book first popped into my head in 2008. I had been talking about my experiences with family and friend and other military families. It wasn't until after that first speech that I realized the gravity of my words. I got to tell all these people the things I had needed to hear for years. You're not alone, strange, or out of the ordinary! You're going to be fine! Your experiences have made you an extraordinary person! It was a great feeling to pass on that message.

A woman came up to me afterward saying she just *knew* what I was talking about. She told me, "Yes! That's exactly what happened to me!" Friends and family distancing themselves, the lonely nights, the crushing responsibility. She felt as though someone truly understood her and felt her pain.

We had really connected over these shared experiences. It felt so good to let others know they weren't the only ones going through these things. Here in front of me was a community of homefront warriors whose collective trials and tribulations had made them the heroes they were that day. People kept telling me, "You should write a book!" Other military spouses egged me on over the coming years, reassuring me I'd be giving their struggles a voice. But I was never really sold on the idea. I figured some other person would come forward to tell their story. *It would probably be better than mine*, I thought. *No one would want to hear about all this, would they?*

After Jon and I separated, it seemed like the window of opportunity to share my story was gone for good. *That's it*, I thought. *I can't tell my story if there isn't a happy ending.* But a friend of mine thought differently.

"That's why you *have* to write it!" she argued. "Maybe this will help change the ending of someone else's story." I knew deep down she was right. True, things hadn't worked out perfectly between Jon and me. We're still discovering who we are and where our lives are taking us. Our families are still close and our kids still have two parents. But this story is far from over.

I realize now that happy endings aren't just series of pleasant events that bookend a challenging time in life. They're rarely like the endings in movies and almost never go the way you want. You're also never guaranteed one. But I think that's a good thing. A happy ending isn't something you're handed at the end of the day. It's something you have to work at each and every day. A happy ending is what you make for yourself. I hope this book is the beginning of your own happily ever after. I know I'm still writing mine.

GREATEST LESSON OF THEM ALL

Throughout this entire experience, I learned one very important thing—it's okay to have needs. Humans are social creatures and are hardwired to connect with others. One of the greatest needs of any homefront warrior is being heard and understood. If we can receive that, nothing will keep us down for long. Just keep in mind, it may take several different types of people to really understand each facet of your struggle.

I was so lucky to have my family nearby when Jon was away, and I was equally lucky to have such wonderful friends. It took their combined efforts to listen to and understand what I was going through. It's important for all homefront warriors to surround themselves and their families with a caring community. Preston needed a father figure, Mary Louise needed time with her mom, and I needed peace, quiet, and reassurance that everything was going to be fine. It was okay that I couldn't provide all these things all the time. It's okay to ask for and receive help from caring individuals around you. It takes real strength to do that.

So what are your needs? It's good to recognize them, especially before a major event such as a soldier's deployment. Do you need a sanctuary—a place to refresh your mind and be at peace? Do you need people around all the time to remind you that you're not alone? Do you need one good friend who really gets you? Give yourself permission to need all of these things and more. It's okay, really. I did not think about these things during those fifteen months. I had it in my mind that I was the lone homefront warrior. I thought it was my sole responsibility to suck it up and get to work. I didn't realize the support group I had waiting in the ranks the entire time.

LOVING REMINDERS

One thing I cannot stress enough is *plan ahead with your family*. When you sit down and talk with your soldier about each of your needs, you can help pinpoint each other's strengths and weaknesses. You can tell yourself you'll be fine until you're blue in the face, but nobody will be better at looking out for your needs than your soldier. Trust each other. Be honest with each other. And for heaven's sake, get your kids involved. You don't have to scare them with the ugliness of the world, but when your soldier leaves, everyone in your family will be affected, including them.

Set up times for rest and relaxation. Plan vacations or days off at home to catch up on housework. Ask friends and family to check in every week or so. Schedule meetings with your pastor and nights out on the town. Don't forget to plan for the homecoming as well. Set up an appointment with a counseling service, even if you think you won't need it. Plan a night with the kids to show your soldier's pictures and encourage them to ask questions. Sit down with your soldier and talk through each other's experiences. There's only so much you can convey over the phone and in letters. Make the effort to understand one another.

Above all, be there for each other in your planning ahead. When you make your soldier's life and your homefront warrior's life easier, you're being present for them even when you can't be there. It's the next best thing to actually having them home.

DOG TAGS

Growing up, you could always tell which families had soldiers abroad by the yellow ribbons in the trees in their front yards. I always thought that was a great way to identify military households; that way, you could go up and thank them for their sacrifice. I wanted to do something like that to bring awareness to a homefront warrior's struggles.

I remember when I started telling my story publicly, I had found my dad's old dog tags. I wore them during every talk, and it got me thinking of the service and sacrifice they represented. Afterward, I went to my parents' house to present them to my dad. "This is never coming off," he told me through his tears. That was a very special day for both of us.

When I began putting this book together, I wanted a way for spouses and kids to represent their soldiers and their own service as military families. I got the idea to make up these cool dog tags with the words "Homefront Warrior" painted on them. I got a friend's son, Mason Burke, to design a logo and then had a bunch printed up. I still love handing them out to homefront warriors I meet around the country. I want them all to be reminded of their duty and sacrifice and to feel pride in wearing them. My hope is that these homefront-warrior dog tags can be like those yellow ribbons and raise awareness among civilians so that people can thank them.

JOIN THE FIGHT

I know recognition made a world of difference to me. There were countless times when I wondered if what I was doing mattered to anyone. But the smallest gesture is all it ever took to lift my spirits. For those of you with homefront warriors in your community, know that the best things you can do for them are always free. A phone call, a hug, a moment of your time to listen—these are the best ways to show your appreciation.

If you're feeling especially generous, I recommend going out and meeting a need without asking. Bring a family some groceries, mow someone's lawn. There are tons of great local charities that cater to military families. Telling a military spouse to "let me know if you need anything" may seem like a polite thing to say, but in reality, it just puts another burden on them. If you really want to support a homefront warrior, don't ask—show. Take someone out to lunch, offer to pick up kids, arrange a babysitter. It's incredible how meaningful it is when someone goes out of their way to make your life easier.

I hope that these ideas inspire you to make a difference in someone's life. To my fellow homefront warriors, I hope my story spoke to you in some way. Whether you felt some sense of understanding or learned something helpful, I hope you know how much I appreciate what you do. You are all courageous, amazing people. You and your soldiers are what make this nation great. I wish each of you peace, strength, and blessings in your life.

ABOUT THE AUTHOR

Chantel Olson is an author, speaker and coach whose mission is to bring awareness to the "Home Front Warriors," the spouses, children, parents, etc. left at home when their loved one is serving in the military.

Chantel also wanted to find a way to honor the Home Front Warriors who deal with the absence of a family member while they serve in the military. "I designed a dog tag that represents the families or Home front Warriors," she said. "They are serving our country too, just in a different way."

Along with her speaking, coaching and writing, Chantel is also a Broker Associate for RE/MAX Professionals, Inc. in Sioux Falls where she specializes in helping Military members, their families, first time home buyers, move up buyers, and the elderly making their Real Estate dreams come true.

Chantel is a native of South Dakota and a mother of 2 children. She knows the ins and outs of balancing her demanding job and taking the time to make family a priority. Going to Baseball, Softball, Football, and Hockey games for her kids is the highlight of her life.

She is also a firm believer in giving back to the community and volunteering. Chantel is a member of the Sons of Norway, on the board of the Tea Housing and Redevelopment Committee, active in her church, and raises money for the Children's Miracle Network. In her free time, she enjoys spending time with her family, four wheeling, cooking, outdoor activities, and being spontaneous with her kids.

Connect with Chantel:

Web: chantelinspires.com

Phone: (605) 376-9697

Email: chantel@chantelinspires.com

Facebook: facebook.com/chantelinspires/

Instagram: instagram.com/chantelinspires/

Twitter: @chantellouise16

www.ingramcontent.com/pod-product-compliance
Lightning Source LLC
Chambersburg PA
CBHW071353090426
42738CB00012B/3100